ANTHONY POWELL

ANTHONY POWELL

by

BERNARD BERGONZI

Edited by Ian Scott-Kilvert

PUBLISHED FOR
THE BRITISH COUNCIL
BY LONGMAN GROUP LTD

LONGMAN GROUP LTD
Longman House, Burnt Mill, Harlow, Essex

*Associated companies, branches and
representatives throughout the world*

*First published 1962
Revised and enlarged edition 1971*
©Bernard Bergonzi 1962, 1971

*Printed in Great Britain by
F. Mildner & Sons, London, EC1*

SBN O 582 01222 8

ANTHONY POWELL

SOME novelists achieve an instant fame with their first book, and spend the rest of their lives failing to live up to that early promise. Anthony Powell's reputation has developed in quite the opposite way, in a slow and deliberate fashion over forty years, from fairly obscure beginnings to a point where he is now widely regarded as one of the finest living English novelists. Powell was born in 1905 and educated at Eton and Oxford, and he published his first novel, *Afternoon Men*, in 1931. It did not arouse much interest, and was followed by four more novels between 1932 and 1939. During the Second World War Powell served in the army and wrote no more fiction, but he made a study of the seventeenth-century antiquarian John Aubrey, and brought out a biography of Aubrey in 1948 and an edition of Aubrey's *Brief Lives* in the following year. Then, in 1951, he published *A Question of Upbringing*, the first volume of *The Music of Time*, the long novel-sequence on which his reputation largely rests. The whole work is intended to fill twelve volumes, of which ten had appeared by 1971.

Afternoon Men can be placed with Evelyn Waugh's *Decline and Fall* as one of the few outstanding first novels to appear in England during the twenties and thirties. Both Powell and Waugh were satirically interested in the London circles, partly fashionable and partly artistic, that had been more cheerfully described and exposed in the early novels of Aldous Huxley. Yet Waugh is more cruel, hysterical and gay; Powell is a detached but sympathetic observer, delineating human folly with the calm of an anthropological field-worker. *Afternoon Men* is pitched in a uniformly minor key; it is a comic masterpiece which avoids extravagance, and achieves its effects by a relentless laconic wit and a stylized manner that looks like artlessness. The danger is that apparent flatness can be mistaken for the real thing, and *Afternoon Men* has never had the recognition it deserves. In this novel Powell first established the fictional territory that he has made peculiarly his own, where several social groups overlap and intersect: writers, artists, journalists and film-makers; professional people with vaguely bohemian tastes; undisguised layabouts, and members of the lesser aristocracy. As Walter Allen has said, Powell's world can be located geographically and spiritually at the point where Mayfair meets Soho. Atwater, the dim but likeable hero of *Afternoon Men*, works in a museum, and the serious side of the story concerns his unsuccessful love affair with Susan Nunnery, who leaves him for a wealthier man; but the comic aspect arises from Atwater's friendship with the painters Pringle and Barlow and their eccentric associates. *Afternoon Men* already contains the essence of Powell's fictional method. There is, first, his preoccupation with style as a mode of mediating and recreating experience; he is not a 'stylist' in the sense of writing poetic prose or seeking colourful verbal effects, but in the novels of the thirties and again in *The Music of Time* Powell achieves a stylistic manner that matches his particular subject-matter. The process is apparent in the opening pages of *Afternoon Men*, where the syntax conveys a sense of experience fragmented into countless disparate units, which are only barely connected (the scene is a London drinking club):

Atwater did not answer. He read a newspaper that someone had left on the table. He read the comic strip and later the column headed 'Titled Woman in Motor Tragedy'. He was a weedy-looking young man with straw-coloured hair and rather long legs, who had failed twice for the Foreign Office. He sometimes wore tortoiseshell-rimmed spectacles to correct a slight squint, and through influence had recently got a job in a museum. His father was a retired civil servant who lived in Essex, where he and his wife kept a chicken farm.

'How long has this place been open?' said Pringle.

'Not long. Everybody comes here.'

'Do they?'

'Mostly.'

This clipped, laconic style occurs throughout *Afternoon Men* and Powell's second novel, *Venusberg* (1932), both works which dwell on the absurdity of human attempts to form genuine relationships. Later in the thirties Powell's style changed; the sentences became longer and the syntax more elaborate, and in *The Music of Time* he writes in a way quite unlike *Afternoon Men*: a complicated, leisurely, reflective and analytical manner, which unsympathetic readers have found merely long-winded. Yet whereas the style of Powell's first two novels had effectively rendered the comic disparity and randomness of experience as it unfolds moment by moment, in *The Music of Time*, Powell is attempting to make aesthetic sense of a lifetime of vanished experiences, to understand them and draw out the significances that were hidden at the time. Powell seems no more convinced in the sequence than he was in the early novels that order and coherence are actually part of reality, but he is prepared to allow that they may appear in the verbal patterning that the novelist imposes on his material, so that style is a necessary principle of order.

The other major aspect of Powell's method that is already quite apparent in *Afternoon Men* is his preoccupation with anecdote and gossip. To some extent such an interest is an essential part of any novelist's equipment, for he is nothing if he is not both a collector and a teller of stories. But Powell's sense of anecdote is remarkably well developed. Thus in *Afternoon Men* one of the unifying motifs in the story consists of recurring references to an absent friend of the principal characters, who never appears but is often spoken of:

'. . . William has had a letter from Undershaft. He's in New York, living with an Annamite and playing the piano.'

'Is he making any money?'

'Doing very well, he says.'

In Powell's view of life such anecdotal allusions are a way of bringing the various strands together, and if the stories are already familiar to those recounting them they provide a welcome sense of assurance in a world without fixed points of reference:

> Pringle had been in pretty good form all day. Barlow said:
> 'What's come over him? It's like when one of the critics said there was a quality of originality about his treatment of water.'
> 'When he rang up Pauline de Chabran at Claridge's?' said Atwater.
> 'The week he told Mrs Beamish her parties were the worst in Europe.'
> 'But he's never been to one.'
> 'That was what made her so angry.' said Barlow.

The anecdotal method is used in a far more extensive but not essentially different way in *The Music of Time*, which is, among other things, a vast, expanding collection of anecdotes about the innumerable people who move in and out of the life of the narrator Nicholas Jenkins, from childhood to middle age. Some are as brief and fragmentary as those in *Afternoon Men*, while others are very long and circumstantial, like Nicholas Jenkins' childhood memory of the dramatic events one Sunday in the summer of 1914, involving his father's cook, Albert, a female servant called Billson, and the visiting General Conyers, which takes up the first seventy pages of *The Kindly Ones* (Vol. VI of *The Music of Time*). This superb piece of writing, one of the great achievements of the whole sequence, contains within itself fragments of small-scale anecdote:

> 'Bertha Conyers has such an amusing way of putting things,' my mother would say. 'But I really don't believe all her stories, especially the one about Mrs Asquith and the man who asked her if she danced the tango.'

Although *The Music of Time* is Powell's major achievement, *Afternoon Men* is, within its far smaller compass, his most sustainedly brilliant book, and remains an endlessly rewarding piece of comic fiction. If it anatomizes a between-wars world of futility and boredom, it does so with calm geniality, and with no sense of moral indignation or metaphysical anguish. In Powell's vision of reality, the comic form remains a permanent assertion of human value, however shabby the behaviour it renders. Although Powell's sense of the absurd is unsurpassed, it is always closer to the purely comic than to the existential. Consider, for instance, the loveless sexual union of Atwater and a girl called Lola, where Powell makes a deliberate and effective departure from the laconic stylistic norm of *Afternoon Men*:

Slowly, but very deliberately, the brooding edifice of seduction, creaking and incongruous, came into being, a vast Heath Robinson mechanism, dually controlled by them and lumbering gloomily down vistas of triteness. With a sort of heavy-fisted dexterity the mutually adapted emotions of each of them became synchronised, until the unavoidable anti-climax was at hand. Later they dined at a restaurant quite near the flat.

Or there is the even more startling shift of style, when one of the lesser characters, a sad, unsuccessful young journalist called Fotheringham, suddenly launches into a long wordy tirade about 'this mad, chaotic armageddon, this frenzied, febrile striving which we, you and I, know life to be', which turns into a page-long sentence of ever increasing syntactical complexity, until Fotheringham finally loses the thread of what he is trying to say. Devoted admirers of *Afternoon Men* will have their favourite episodes; one of my own is the section in which Pringle, who has been entertaining a party of friends in his cottage near the sea, has a row with his girl and decides to commit suicide. He leaves a note announcing his intention of not returning from bathing. A few hours later, after his friends have been in much distress, he is discovered in fisherman's clothes, looking round the cottage for the note. He explains that he changed his mind and was picked up by some fishermen. A little later, when one of the fishermen comes to claim his clothes, an argument arises between Pringle and his friends about how much he should give the man for saving him; ten shillings seems too little, and a pound too much, so he compromises with fifteen shillings. The man simply says 'Tar' when handed the money, and Pringle observes, 'That was obviously the right sum.'

Venusberg, Powell's next novel, is stylistically similar to *Afternoon Men*, and its hero, Lushington, is another likeable, ineffectual young man. The book describes his adventures in a small Baltic capital where he is sent as a journalist; he has an unhappy love affair with the wife of a professor, and runs into a variety of exotic local characters. There are a number of entertaining scenes, but the novel is for the most part slight and over-episodic, with little of the comic brilliance of *Afternoon Men*. It ends on a note of sudden arbitrary violence and death, that is rather beyond Powell's abilities to make convincing. His third novel, *From a View to a Death* (1933), is a good deal more interesting. It is set in an English village, a society of declining county families, who are disturbed by the advent of an ambitious and social-climbing young artist called Zouch, a vulgar and unattractive figure, who nevertheless has a degree of energy and drive that is lacking in the society he is trying to penetrate. Zouch has, in fact, some slight affinity with Stendhal's Julien Sorel, and like Julien comes to an abrupt and violent end; certainly Stendhal has always been an author much admired by Powell, and figures of boundless will-power are endlessly fascinating to him. In *From a View to a Death* the prose is less economical and more explicit than in *Afternoon Men*, and the novel as a whole has greater solidity and less sharpness. It displays a recognizable segment of English society in some depth, whereas the first two novels had concentrated on the antics and collisions of individual characters; to this extent Powell is already looking forward to the method of *The Music of Time*. Although parts of the book are as funny as anything that Powell has written, its total impact is by no means wholly comic; the novel is pervaded by an atmosphere of lassitude and frustration which recalls other, more socially-committed writings of the nineteen-thirties. It seems that in this novel Powell was trying to convey his own sense of what W. H. Auden in an exactly contemporary work, *The Orators*, called 'this England of ours where no-one is really well', where even a richly grotesque character like Major Fosdick, who likes dressing up in women's clothes in the privacy of his study, is not merely a comic figure but a sign of the malaise of his class.

Yet if in *From a View to a Death* Powell, like many other English writers of that time, reflected on the condition of his society, in his next novel he turned away to the pursuit of pure farce. *Agents and Patients* (1936) is, to my mind, the weakest of Powell's pre-war novels, and the one where he most directly invites comparison, to his disadvantage, with the early Evelyn Waugh. *Agents and Patients* is about two hard-up adventurers, Maltravers, a film-writer, and Chipchase, an art-critic and amateur psychoanalyst, who devote themselves to financially exploiting a rich, Candide-like young man called Blore-Smith, who, at the start of the novel, has more money than sense, though by the end of it he has acquired wisdom the hard way. The story moves in a brisk, picaresque fashion across Europe and contains some lively passages set in a German film studio, no doubt embodying some of Powell's own experiences as a script-writer in the thirties.

After a three-year interval Powell published his last pre-war novel, *What's Become of Waring?* (1939). It takes its title from a poem by Browning, and describes the attempt to discover a popular author called T. T. Waring who has never been seen in the flesh by his publisher, and who is one day reported to be dead. Powell works out this quite fruitful idea in an unusually tightly-plotted work, which is full of entertaining incident, though lacking in real inventiveness. In the perspective of Powell's later work, *What's Become of Waring?* is particularly interesting for its evident anticipations of the manner of *The Music of Time*. The story is told in the first person by an unnamed young publisher, who shares one of Powell's abiding interests by trying to write a book called *Stendhal: and Some Thoughts on*

Violence. His account of the hunt for the semi-mythical Waring is very reminiscent of Nicholas Jenkins; he, too, has a cool, unobtrusive but sharply observant way of noting the oddities of human behaviour, in a style that is more elaborate than anything that Powell had so far attempted. His account of an old acquaintance, General Pimley, is characteristic:

A man in shirt-sleeves whom I recognised as General Pimley was mowing the lawn. He was much as I remembered him, slight and wizened, with a dome-shaped head across the brow of which ran three heavily marked lines that gave him the worried humorous expression of an actor wearing a false forehead. When he saw us he hunched his shoulders and swung forward ape-like over the mower. His posture and the fact that he had removed his collar and tie heightened the illusion that he was a sad clown about to perform a tumbling act to entertain a not very appreciative audience.

Nicholas Jenkins, also, is given to similarly elaborate theatrical metaphors and similes, and to observing human life as a serio-comic spectacle or series of performances: on a later and more formal occasion, General Pimley, this time wearing an opera-hat and black overcoat, is said to look like an 'immensely distinguished conjuror'. On the last page of *What's Become of Waring?* the narrator sets down his thoughts during a sleepless night; he broods restlessly on the nature of power, and the different ways in which the characters of the story have pursued it. And here we have a direct and striking anticipation of *The Music of Time*, a work in which many people have a taste for power, and live by the exercise of the will: Widmerpool, Sillery, Sir Magnus Donners, J. G. Quiggin, Alf Warminster, Tuffy Weedon, Idwal Kedward, a famous British Field-Marshal. At the point when he had concluded *What's Become of Waring?* Powell seemed ready to have gone on to *The Music of Time*, or some similar work. But the Second World War intervened, and it was to be twelve years before he returned to fiction.

II

In a recent interview[1] Powell described the spirit in which he made a study of John Aubrey during the war years:

I thought that I wouldn't be able to write a novel immediately after the war if I survived, and therefore did start making notes on John Aubrey, the seventeenth-century antiquary, with the idea of writing a book on Aubrey. During my leaves I did quite a lot of work on that, and at the end of the war I produced this book which was simply a question of plugging away at a lot of historical material—and then I found that somehow did the trick, and one was in a mood to write a novel again.

Powell's transitional study of Aubrey is very relevant to *The Music of Time*, where the anecdotal method and the endless interest in the oddities of human behaviour and character indicate a cast of mind akin to Aubrey's own. Indeed, Powell has referred to Aubrey's 'presentation of life as a picture crowded with odd figures, occupying themselves in unexpected and inexplicable pursuits', words which could appropriately be applied to *The Music of Time*.

In the same interview Powell discussed the genesis of his sequence:

After the war I thought a good deal about my writing—about writing novels in general—and I came to the conclusion that as I had already written the 80,000 sort of novel now I was going to settle down to do something much longer—generally approach the thing more thoroughly. If you wrote a lot more novels, each one separate, you would be losing a lot from the ideas you put into them by not connecting those ideas, if you see what I mean. And therefore I thought one would do best to settle down to write one really long novel. I hadn't then decided that it would necessarily be twelve volumes, but I did think it would be a great number of volumes, and that one would, so to speak, pick up in that way all you lose by ending a book and starting again with a lot of entirely new characters.

[1] Recorded in *Summary*, Autumn 1970.

A Question of Upbringing opens with a long, detailed description of a group of workmen warming themselves round a coke brazier with snow falling on them. This image releases in Jenkins's mind a number of potent suggestions; he thinks of the ancient world—'legionaries in sheepskin warming themselves at a brazier: mountain altars where offerings glow between wintry pillars; centaurs with torches cantering beside a frozen sea'—and then, by further association, of a painting by Poussin called 'A Dance to the Music of Time':

in which the Seasons, hand in hand and facing outward, tread in rhythm to the notes of the lyre that the winged and naked greybeard plays. The image of Time brought thoughts of mortality: of human beings, facing outward like the Seasons, moving hand in hand in intricate measure: stepping slowly, methodically, sometimes a trifle awkwardly, in evolutions that take recognisable shape: or breaking into seemingly meaningless gyrations, while partners disappear only to reappear again, once more giving pattern to the spectacle: unable to control the melody, unable, perhaps, to control the steps of the dance. Classical associations made me think, too, of days at school, where so many forces, hitherto unfamiliar, had become in due course uncompromisingly clear.

It is characteristic of Jenkins that experience presents itself to him in strongly visual terms, either in recalling actual, familiar works of art; or as formal *tableaux* of characters that suggest both painting and theatrical performance. There is a striking instance in *The Kindly Ones* in which Sir Magnus Donners, to gratify some private taste of his own, induces his guests to dress up as figures representing the Seven Deadly Sins: the resulting spectacle offers full scope to Jenkins's narrative gifts. The dance so graphically imagined at the beginning of *A Question of Upbringing* is a comprehensive emblem of the action of Powell's long novel, where a large number of characters do indeed weave in and out of each other's lives, disappearing and reappearing in unexpected ways. Or at least it is true of the earlier volumes of *The Music of Time* where Nicholas Jenkins is a young man making his way in the world, moving through the complex, interrelated circles of fashionable and bohemian life in London, and steadily enlarging his groups of acquaintances. But in the later volumes, the number of the dancers has been much reduced, by old age or other intrusions of mortality, and above all by war. In the iconography of modern art and literature, the dance is an image of freedom from time, change and decay: as Powell's novel moves towards its conclusion, and Nicholas Jenkins becomes middle-aged, the carefree absorption of the dancers has become vulnerable to the depredations of history and mortality, so that the dance seems less adequate as a structural principle.

Powell intends the twelve volumes of *The Music of Time* to fall into four constituent trilogies. The first of them is composed of *A Question of Upbringing*, *A Buyer's Market* (1952) and *The Acceptance World* (1955). In *A Question of Upbringing* we first meet Nicholas Jenkins in 1921 as a schoolboy at Eton, and then move on to his days as an undergraduate at Oxford (neither institution is named, but clearly identifiable): in this novel we meet three school-fellows of Nicholas, who are to remain central characters in much of *The Music of Time*: Charles Stringham, witty, elegant, self-assured, though with an underlying melancholia that later turns him into an alcoholic; the raffish, womanizing Peter Templer, whom Stringham warns, 'if you're not careful you will suffer the awful fate of the man who always knows the right clothes to wear and the right shop to buy them at', a phrase that exactly sums up Templer's worldliness, though it does not anticipate the far grimmer fate that will descend on Templer during the Second World War. And there is, above all, Widmerpool, one of the great characters of modern fiction, whom we encounter in the opening chapter: Jenkins is returning from a walk on a winter afternoon, when an ungainly boy lumbers past in sweater and running shoes, returning from a solitary run. It is Widmerpool, who was already notorious

at the school as an oddity; but, says Jenkins, it was at this
point that 'Widmerpool, fairly heavily built, thick lips and
metal-rimmed spectacles giving his face as usual an aggrieved
expression, first took coherent form in my mind.' Widmerpool is at this point no more than a figure of fun: 'That boy
will be the death of me,' remarks Stringham, but twenty
years later his words come literally true.

In *A Buyer's Market* Jenkins wanders through London
society in the late twenties. He and Widmerpool are both
in love with Barbara Goring, a pretty but irresponsible
girl who subjects Widmerpool to a spectacular humiliation
at a dance. Remarking, 'Why are you so sour tonight?
You need some sweetening,' she picks up a heavy sugar
castor, meaning to sprinkle a few grains over him. But the
top falls off, and Widmerpool is covered in a cascade of
sugar. It is one of the few overtly farcical pieces of action
in *The Music of Time*, and the absurdity is heightened by the
slow-motion description and Powell's habitual sense of the
visually grotesque:

Widmerpool's rather sparse hair had been liberally greased with a
dressing—the sweetish smell of which I remembered as somewhat
disagreeable when applied in France—this lubricant retaining the grains
of sugar, which, as they adhered thickly to his skull, gave him the
appearance of having turned white with shock at a single stroke;
which, judging by what could be seen of his expression, he might very
well in reality have done underneath the glittering incrustations that
enveloped his head and shoulders.

But it takes more than such a débâcle to depress Widmerpool's energies for long. *The Acceptance World* carries the
story on into the early nineteen-thirties, when the carefree
twenties give way to a phase of leftist politics and social
commitment. Nicholas remains as detached as ever, but he
is for a time involved with St John Clarke, an elderly
novelist who has taken up Marxism late in life, and an
Oxford acquaintance, J. G. Quiggin, an able literary critic
and left-wing activist who frequently asserts his humble
origins, and is a forerunner of the angry young men of the

nineteen-fifties. Widmerpool is rising in the 'acceptance
world' of credit finance, and Nicholas has his first serious
love affair, with Templer's cousin, Jean Duport.

The second trilogy comprises *At Lady Molly's* (1957),
Casanova's Chinese Restaurant (1960) and *The Kindly Ones*
(1962), and covers the middle and late thirties. It is a period
of consolidation in Nicholas Jenkins's life: he establishes a
modest reputation for himself as a novelist, and marries
Lady Isobel Tolland, whose many relations bring a whole
host of new acquaintances into his life. Isobel's brother is
the 'red earl', Erridge, or Lord Warminster, known as 'Alf'
to his intimates, a marvellously drawn aristocratic eccentric,
and one of Powell's many characters who aspire to live by
the power of the will, though in practice his political
aspirations come to nothing. If Nicholas marries, so do
several other characters, not always successfully, and the
theme of marriage is dominant in *Casanova's Chinese
Restaurant*. In *At Lady Molly's* even the self-absorbed
Widmerpool had contemplated marrying Mrs Mildred
Haycock, a sophisticated widow with two children, several
years older than himself; he circumspectly asks Jenkins
whether his fiancée might not expect him to sleep with her
before the marriage:

'In fact my fiancée—Mildred, that is—might even expect such a
suggestion?'
'Well, yes, from what you say.'
'Might even regard it as *usage du monde*?'
'Quite possible.'
Then Widmerpool sniggered. For some reason I was conscious of
embarrassment, even of annoyance. The problem could be treated as
it were, clinically, or humorously; a combination of the two approaches
was distasteful. I had the impression that the question of how he should
behave worried him more on account of the figure he cut in the eyes of
Mrs Haycock than because his passion could not be curbed.

This passage shows how the laconic dialogue of *Afternoon
Men* has come to carry a wide range of social nuance, while
Nicholas's own cool reflection illustrates his capacity for

precisely delineating human folly and self-deception.
Widmerpool makes the experiment, which is not a success,
and the engagement is shortly broken off. It is worth
noting, incidentally, that though Nicholas has no difficulty
in seeing through Widmerpool he still continues to like him,
or at least to find his company perfectly supportable,
unlike many others of their acquaintance.

Casanova's Chinese Restaurant is a more sombre work
than any of the preceding volumes. The rise of fascism in
Europe and the Civil War in Spain cast a shadow, while
English society is shaken by the crisis over the abdication of
King Edward VIII. Powell gives little space to direct
discussion of these events, but he shows his characters as
clearly responding to the public issues of the time. At the
same time their lives are noticeably less carefree than in the
earlier volumes. The embittered music critic, Maclintick,
commits suicide, while another new friend of Nicholas, the
composer Moreland and his wife have a baby which dies.
Nicholas's wife has a miscarriage, and marriages seem to be
falling apart on all sides. His own married life seems to be
stable and happy, though he says very little about it, and
Powell has been criticized for this reticence, for making his
narrator tell us so much about other people's lives and so
little about his own. Yet there is an important passage in
which Nicholas dwells on the impossibility of giving a
convincing account of marriage from the inside:

A future marriage, or a past one, may be investigated and explained
in terms of writing by one of its parties, but it is doubtful whether an
existing marriage can ever be described directly in the first person and
convey a sense of reality. Even those writers who suggest some of the
substance of married life best, stylise heavily, losing the subtlety of the
relationship at the price of a few accurately recorded, but isolated,
aspects. To think at all objectively about one's own marriage is impossible,
while a balanced view of other people's marriage is almost equally
hard to achieve with so much information available, so little to be
believed. Objectivity is not, of course, everything in writing; but
even casting objectivity aside, the difficulties of presenting marriage are

inordinate. Its forms are at once so varied, yet so constant, providing a kaleidoscope, the colours of which are always changing, always the same. The moods of a love affair, the contradictions of friendship, the jealousy of business partners, the fellow feeling of opposed commanders in total war, these are all in their way to be charted. Marriage, partaking of such—and a thousand more—dual antagonisms and participations, finally defies definition.

The Kindly Ones begins with an extended memory from Nicholas's childhood of the eve of war in 1914; it returns to the present reality of 1939 and the death of his Uncle Giles, a rather disreputable figure who had made a variety of mysterious but portentous appearances in Nicholas's early life; a few days later, the Second World War breaks out, bringing to an end both a phase of history, and the early manhood of the narrator.

III

The third trilogy, made up of *The Valley of Bones* (1964), *The Soldier's Art* (1966), and *The Military Philosophers* (1968), covers the six years of war and the narrator's military service, first as a rather over-age subaltern with a Welsh regiment stationed in Northern Ireland, then as an officer with the Intelligence Corps in London, engaged on liaison duties with the allied armies. Nicholas continues to make new friends, though at nothing like the rate of his early life, and several old and familiar faces disappear. His wife's aunt, Lady Molly Jeavons, his sister-in-law Priscilla and her husband, Chips Lovell, are killed in the bombing of London. Stringham dies as a prisoner of the Japanese, having been sent to the Far East by Widmerpool, now his military superior, and Peter Templer is killed in mysterious circumstances on a secret mission in German-occupied Europe. On the other hand, Widmerpool rises steadily in the military hierarchy. Nicholas becomes a father, and we leave him after the Victory Service in St Paul's in 1945. *Books do Furnish a Room* (1971), the first volume of the final trilogy, covers the years from 1945 to 1947. Nicholas Jenkins picks up the threads of civilian life by writing a book on Robert Burton, author of *The Anatomy of Melancholy*—an evident parallel to Powell's own study of John Aubrey—and contributing to a small literary magazine called *Fission*. Powell brings together many figures in the chronicle who have survived the war, in some cases going back to Jenkins's childhood; Widmerpool is prominent as a Labour MP, and at the end of the book has achieved minor office in the Attlee government. He is married to Charles Stringham's niece, Pamela, a beautiful, neurotic and consistently destructive girl. For the first time his customary ebullience is somewhat dented, and he shows an unaccustomed capacity for suffering. The book is both serenely comic and gently elegiac. It catches a particular moment in recent history; a short-lived phase of literary activity and aspiration in a London that still showed all the physical destruction and decay of six years of war.

This bare outline of *The Music of Time* will not convey anything of its true flavour, particularly of its intricacy and multiplicity of anecdote, and the immense range of characters, major or minor, that must run into several hundred. The appeal of Powell's work is of a remarkably simple kind: to our love of story-telling and gossip and anecdote. It provokes, and partially assuages, an intense but uncommitted curiosity about humanity, and a traditionally English interest in 'characters' and eccentrics. It is possible for addicted readers of *The Music of Time*, eagerly awaiting the appearance of the next volume, to become caught up in the antics and interrelations (particularly the sexual alliances and severances) of Powell's characters just as if, in the time-honoured phrase, 'they were real people'. This, one imagines, is precisely how innumerable Victorian readers felt about the work of the great novelists of their age as they published their books in monthly parts.

Powell writes, admittedly, of a fairly small world, even though it is densely populated; his vision of it is in the central tradition of English social comedy that derives from Jane Austen. He is totally intimate with this world, and yet is invariably detached enough to catch with dazzling accuracy the minutest aspect of its manners. As Lionel Trilling has written, 'one of the things which makes for substantiality of character in the novel is precisely the notation of manners, that is to say, of class traits modified by personality.' Consider for instance in *A Question of Upbringing*, the appearance of Stringham's stepfather, the 'polo-playing sailor', Buster Foxe, first observed cleaning a cigarette-holder with the end of a matchstick:

He was tall, and at once struck me as surprisingly young; with the slightly drawn expression that one recognises in later life as the face of a man who does himself pretty well, while not ceasing to take plenty of exercise. His turn-out was emphatically excellent, and he diffused waves of personality, strong, chilling gusts of icy air, a protective element that threatened to freeze into rigidity all who came through the door, before they could approach him nearer.

'Hallo, you fellows,' he said, without looking up from his cigarette-holder, at which he appeared to be sneering, as if this object were not nearly valuable enough to presume to belong to him.

In *The Kindly Ones* there is a fine instance of Nicholas Jenkins's awareness of the typical in the idiosyncratic when he describes Sir Magnus Donners's method of shaking hands:

giving, when he reached me, that curious pump-handle motion to his handshake, terminated by a sudden upward jerk (as if suddenly shutting off from the main valuable current of good will, of which not a volt too much must be expended), a form of greeting common to many persons with a long habit of public life.

The segment of English society that Powell writes about is one in which, in a loose sense, everyone knows everyone else, where Oxford, Cambridge, the public schools, all have connexions with the principal London foci of intellectual, professional and business life, to form a fairly coherent network. This is less so today than it was in the twenties and thirties; nevertheless, it is still true that a surprising number of English people in different walks of life know each other, or at least know of each other, and links are preserved between disparate circles by a network of friends or relations, or friends of friends. Although *The Music of Time* is full of chance meetings and the discovery of coincidental links between previously unrelated people, none of them seems to strain credulity, since they are typical of the stratum of English life Powell has made his own, where novelistic possibilities lie all around. Not that they can be realized without some degree of effort and difficulty; as Nicholas observes in *The Acceptance World* of his own novel-writing activities:

> Intricacies of social life make English habits unyielding to simplification, while understatement and irony—in which all classes of this island converse—upset the normal emphasis of reported speech.

In his fascinated awareness of these intricacies, his constant sense of the gap between aspiration and achievement, and between appearance and reality, Powell is in the mainstream of English social comedy, where our perception of the world requires a perpetual mild, ironic adjustment. One critic, James Hall, has written about the 'polite surprise' that Nicholas is always displaying at some fresh manifestation of absurdity or unpredictability in his surroundings. For Powell, he suggests, life

> is a series of small shocks to be met with slightly raised eyebrows and the instantaneous question of how it all fits. Above everything else, Nick wants to know within a safe margin of error where he is at any given moment.

This is, I think, an important observation. Although Powell offers us a plenitude of character comparable to one of the great Victorians, his fictional universe, unlike theirs, is not at all solid or stable; we are constantly aware of its inherent fragility and of the uncertainty of Nicholas's relation to it, of his need to know 'where he is at any given moment'. Hence the importance of style, which in *The Music of Time* is a tentacular, analytical, leisurely style, as a means of preserving the narrator's poise and equilibrium. The device is cumulatively successful; as the sequence develops we feel more and more that the one trustworthy point of reference in an endlessly shifting world is the cool, tentative intelligence of Nicholas Jenkins.

Unlike Evelyn Waugh, Powell is not a mythologizer, and there is nothing in his fiction comparable to the romantic image of the doomed gentleman that we find recurring in such novels by Waugh as *A Handful of Dust, Brideshead Revisited,* and *Sword of Honour.* Although Powell is acutely interested in the past, he does not lament it; change and even decay are seen as inevitable and something to be endured with as good a grace as possible, since, whatever happens, life goes on. There are certainly traces of nostalgia in Nicholas's make-up, usually evoked by paintings or buildings, but he never allows them to dominate him. In his attitude to the past, Powell both recalls and differs from Proust. Superficially of course *The Music of Time* is very indebted to Proust's great novel: in its title, its verbal organization, and the kind of life it describes. Indeed, there might be a case for calling it a deliberate 'imitation' of *A la Recherche du Temps Perdu.* Nevertheless, the differences are crucial: unlike Proust's Marcel, Nicholas Jenkins is only occasionally introspective and is far more interested in other people than himself. Nor is Powell much concerned with time itself as an intractable or delusive element; the chronology of *The Music of Time* is straightforward, and, to quote James Hall again, 'Time moves onward as persistently in Nick's story as in Arnold Bennett, and the changes it brings, rather than the possibility of reliving lost experience, interest him.'

Another critic, Arthur Mizener, has acutely described *The Music of Time* as the work of 'an enormously intelligent but completely untheoretical mind.' It is true that Powell

has never resorted to the abstract sustaining principles of
other writers of extended fiction: history for Tolstoy, time
for Proust, or tradition for Waugh. Indeed, he has an
English distaste for ideas and his reliance on anecdote rather
than theme can produce a random, even disorientating
effect. Nevertheless, Powell has a clear sense of history, even
if he lacks a definite or fixed attitude to it. Powell's novel, it
can now be confidently asserted, is a great work of social
comedy, but it undoubtedly describes a shabby and dispirited
society, and one's delight in his characters is sometimes
tempered by a feeling akin to Matthew Arnold's outburst
at the Shelley circle: 'What a set!' In the first two trilogies
Powell is writing about a world still suffering from the
physically and morally traumatic effects of the First World
War, and in a quiet and unembittered way he is continuing
the anatomy of a society in decline embarked on by Ford
Madox Ford in *Parade's End*. Indeed, a critic has written
an essay on *The Music of Time* called 'Chronicle of a Declining Establishment'. But it is easy to over-emphasize this
aspect of Powell's work, and to miss the necessary nuances
of tone in the story as Nicholas Jenkins tells it. *The Music
of Time* is essentially a comedy, and Powell has no time for
myths of catastrophe. Nevertheless, he does, perhaps, allow
himself a few convictions about life, of a kind suggested
by Arthur Mizener, who has pointed to the contrast between
Widmerpool and Stringham as 'a major contrast of
twentieth-century natures'. For Powell, Widmerpool repre-
sents in an unusually pure form the power of the will: he is
insensitive, pompous, socially inept and monstrously
selfish; yet he possesses an almost demonic energy and an
unstoppable urge to succeed. At intervals Nicholas reflects
with reluctant admiration on Widmerpool's prowess, as
when he instantly summons a taxi at a moment of crisis:
'A cab seemed to rise out of the earth at that moment.
Perhaps all action, even summoning a taxi when none is
there, is basically a matter of the will.' Against Widmerpool
and all that he stands for is set the graceful and attractive

but doomed Stringham. Here is how he is described in *A Question of Upbringing*, in one of Powell's characteristic art-historical images:

He was tall and dark, and looked like one of those stiff, sad young men in ruffs, whose long legs take up so much room in sixteenth-century portraits: or perhaps a younger—and far slighter—version of Veronese's Alexander receiving the children of Darius after the Battle of Issus: with the same high forehead and suggestion of hair thinning a bit at the temples. His features certainly seemed to belong to that epoch of painting: the faces in Elizabethan miniatures, lively, obstinate, generous, not very happy, and quite relentless. He was an excellent mimic, and, although he suffered from prolonged fits of melancholy, he talked a lot when one of these splenetic fits was not upon him: and ragged with extraordinary violence when excited.

In the early stages of the novel the elegant Stringham seems an immeasurably superior person to the gross and pompous Widmerpool. But by degrees their relative positions change, as Stringham is undermined by his own weaknesses, becoming for a time an alcoholic and having to be looked after by a former governess, Miss Weedon; while Widmerpool continues inexorably to exert his iron will, despite incidental humiliations. The crucial change in their relationship comes in *The Acceptance World*, where Jenkins and Widmerpool take the drunken Stringham home, and Widmerpool succeeds in getting him into bed by sheer physical force. Mr Mizener has suggested that Powell sees the twentieth century 'as a world nearly transformed by Widmerpools though still haunted by Stringhams'. This was a reasonable comment to make on the early volumes of the sequence, even though it makes Powell seem too consciously elegiac a writer in the manner of Waugh.

Nicholas Jenkins's attitude to Widmerpool is not, in fact, simple; as I have suggested, much as he deplores Widmerpool's behaviour, he always tolerates him and even finds him fascinating: the cool observer and the man who lives by the will seem, indeed, to have a secret affinity for each other and this, rather than the early contrast between

Widmerpool and Stringham, may prove to be the deeper pattern of the whole sequence. Powell is unlike other twentieth-century novelists in having a general affection and even respect for all his characters, no matter how tiresome or obnoxious they may appear in their actions: no-one is condemned for being 'anti-life' or morally corrupt or a social upstart. We are all sinners, he seems to imply, and should not judge one another, and although Powell displays a quintessentially secular caste of mind he regards his creations with an exemplary religious compassion. Underlying the marvellously observed and recorded social comedy of a particular culture and phase of history, there is something more fundamental; the basic human comedy where, as in Chaucer and Rabelais and Shakespeare, folly and weakness and vice are transformed into an unending comic dance.

ANTHONY POWELL

A Select Bibliography

(Place of publication London, unless stated otherwise)

Separate Works:

AFTERNOON MEN (1931). *Novel*
—new edition, 1952.
VENUSBERG (1932). *Novel*
—new edition, 1955.
FROM A VIEW TO A DEATH (1933). *Novel*
AGENTS AND PATIENTS (1936). *Novel*
—new edition, 1955.
WHAT'S BECOME OF WARING? (1939). *Novel*
—new edition, 1953.
JOHN AUBREY AND HIS FRIENDS (1948). *Biography*
—revised edition, 1963.
BRIEF LIVES AND OTHER SELECTED WRITINGS BY JOHN AUBREY, edited
    with an introduction by Anthony Powell (1949). *Biography*
A QUESTION OF UPBRINGING (1951).
A BUYER'S MARKET (1952).
THE ACCEPTANCE WORLD (1955).
AT LADY MOLLY'S (1957).
CASANOVA'S CHINESE RESTAURANT (1960).
THE KINDLY ONES (1962).
THE VALLEY OF BONES (1964).
THE SOLDIER'S ART (1966).
THE MILITARY PHILOSOPHERS (1968).
BOOKS DO FURNISH A ROOM (1971).
Note: The preceding ten novels form part of the sequence *The
    Music of Time.*
THE GARDEN GOD and THE REST I'LL WHISTLE (1971). *Plays*

Some Critical and Other Studies:

'From a Chase to a View', *Times Literary Supplement*, 15 February
    1951.
'The Social Comedy of Anthony Powell', by A. Brownjohn,
    Gemini, Summer 1957.

'A Who's Who of *The Music of Time*', *Time and Tide*, 2 and 9 July 1960.

'From Wauchop to Widmerpool', by J. Brooke, *London Magazine*, September 1960.

'Taken from Life' (an interview), *Twentieth Century*, July 1961.

PUZZLES AND EPIPHANIES: Essays and Reviews 1958–1961, by F. Kermode (1962).

THE TRAGIC COMEDIANS: Seven modern British novelists, by J. Hall; Bloomington, Indiana (1963).

TRADITION AND DREAM: the English and American novel from the twenties to our time, by W. Allen (1964).

THE MODERN WRITER AND HIS WORLD, by G. S. Fraser (1964).

—revised and enlarged edition, 1970, contains most material on Powell,

THE SENSE OF LIFE IN THE MODERN NOVEL, by A. Mizener (1965).

THE WORKING NOVELIST, by V. S. Pritchett (1965).

CRITICAL OCCASIONS, by J. Symons (1966).

'Anthony Powell's *Music of Time*: Chronicle of a Declining Establishment', by J. J. Zigerell, *Twentieth Century Literature*, October 1966.

'Taste of the Old Time', by K. W. Gransden, *Encounter*, December 1966.

'The Art of Horace Isbister, E. Bosworth Deacon and Ralph Barnaby', by M. Glazebrook, *London Magazine*, November 1967.

THE NOVELS OF ANTHONY POWELL, by R. K. Morris; Pittsburgh, Pa. (1968).

'Anthony Powell's Serious Comedy, by W. H. Pritchard, *Massachusetts Review*, Autumn 1969.

SPHERE HISTORY OF LITERATURE IN THE ENGLISH LANGUAGE (1970–)
—Vol. VII, *The Twentieth Century*, ed. B. Bergonzi, contains a chapter by S. Wall entitled 'Aspects of the Novel, 1930–1960'.

'Anthony Powell: a Symposium', *Summary*, Autumn 1970.

ANTHONY POWELL: A Quintet, Sextet and War, by J. Russell; Bloomington, Indiana (1971).

WRITERS AND THEIR WORK

BYRON: Bernard Blackstone
CARLYLE: David Gascoyne
LEWIS CARROLL: Derek Hudson
COLERIDGE: Kathleen Raine
CREEVEY & GREVILLE: J. Richardson
DE QUINCEY: Hugh Sykes Davies
DICKENS: K. J. Fielding
   EARLY NOVELS: T. Blount
   LATER NOVELS: B. Hardy
DISRAELI: Paul Bloomfield
GEORGE ELIOT: Lettice Cooper
FERRIER & GALT: W. M. Parker
FITZGERALD: Joanna Richardson
ELIZABETH GASKELL: Miriam Allott
GISSING: A. C. Ward
THOMAS HARDY: R. A. Scott-James
      and C. Day Lewis
HAZLITT: J. B. Priestley
HOOD: Laurence Brander
G. M. HOPKINS: Geoffrey Grigson
T. H. HUXLEY: William Irvine
KEATS: Edmund Blunden
LAMB: Edmund Blunden
LANDOR: G. Rostrevor Hamilton
EDWARD LEAR: Joanna Richardson
MACAULAY: G. R. Potter
MEREDITH: Phyllis Bartlett
JOHN STUART MILL: M. Cranston
WILLIAM MORRIS: P. Henderson
NEWMAN: J. M. Cameron
PATER: Iain Fletcher
PEACOCK: J. I. M. Stewart
ROSSETTI: Oswald Doughty
CHRISTINA ROSSETTI: G. Battiscombe
RUSKIN: Peter Quennell
SIR WALTER SCOTT: Ian Jack
SHELLEY: G. M. Matthews
SOUTHEY: Geoffrey Carnall
LESLIE STEPHEN: Phyllis Grosskurth
R. L. STEVENSON: G. B. Stern
SWINBURNE: H. J. C. Grierson
TENNYSON: B. C. Southam
THACKERAY: Laurence Brander
FRANCIS THOMPSON: P. Butter
TROLLOPE: Hugh Sykes Davies
OSCAR WILDE: James Laver
WORDSWORTH: Helen Darbishire

Twentieth Century:
CHINUA ACHEBE: A. Ravenscroft
W. H. AUDEN: Richard Hoggart
HILAIRE BELLOC: Renée Haynes
ARNOLD BENNETT: F. Swinnerton
EDMUND BLUNDEN: Alec M. Hardie
ROBERT BRIDGES: J. Sparrow
ROY CAMPBELL: David Wright
JOYCE CARY: Walter Allen
G. K. CHESTERTON: C. Hollis

WINSTON CHURCHILL: John Connell
R. G. COLLINGWOOD: E. W. F. Tomlin
I. COMPTON-BURNETT:
      R. Glynn Grylls
JOSEPH CONRAD: Oliver Warner
WALTER DE LA MARE: K. Hopkins
NORMAN DOUGLAS: Ian Greenlees
LAWRENCE DURRELL: G. S. Fraser
T. S. ELIOT: M. C. Bradbrook
FIRBANK & BETJEMAN: J. Brooke
FORD MADOX FORD: Kenneth Young
E. M. FORSTER: Rex Warner
CHRISTOPHER FRY: Derek Stanford
JOHN GALSWORTHY: R. H. Mottram
WM. GOLDING: Clive Pemberton
ROBERT GRAVES: M. Seymour-Smith
GRAHAM GREENE: Francis Wyndham
L. P. HARTLEY: Paul Bloomfield
A. E. HOUSMAN: Ian Scott-Kilvert
ALDOUS HUXLEY: Jocelyn Brooke
HENRY JAMES: Michael Swan
PAMELA HANSFORD JOHNSON:
      Isabel Quigly
JAMES JOYCE: J. I. M. Stewart
RUDYARD KIPLING: Bonamy Dobrée
D. H. LAWRENCE: Kenneth Young
C. DAY LEWIS: Clifford Dyment
WYNDHAM LEWIS: E. W. F. Tomlin
COMPTON MACKENZIE: K. Young
LOUIS MACNEICE: John Press
KATHERINE MANSFIELD: Ian Gordon
JOHN MASEFIELD: L. A. G. Strong
SOMERSET MAUGHAM: J. Brophy
GEORGE MOORE: A. Norman Jeffares
J. MIDDLETON MURRY: Philip Mairet
SEAN O'CASEY: W. A. Armstrong
GEORGE ORWELL: Tom Hopkinson
JOHN OSBORNE: Simon Trussler
HAROLD PINTER: John Russell Taylor
POETS OF 1939–45 WAR: R. N. Currey
POWYS BROTHERS: R. C. Churchill
J. B. PRIESTLEY: Ivor Brown
HERBERT READ: Francis Berry
FOUR REALIST NOVELISTS: V. Brome
BERNARD SHAW: A. C. Ward
EDITH SITWELL: John Lehmann
KENNETH SLESSOR: C. Semmler
C. P. SNOW: William Cooper
SYNGE & LADY GREGORY: E. Coxhead
DYLAN THOMAS: G. S. Fraser
G. M. TREVELYAN: J. H. Plumb
WAR POETS: 1914–18: E. Blunden
EVELYN WAUGH: Christopher Hollis
H. G. WELLS: Montgomery Belgion
PATRICK WHITE: R. F. Brissenden
ANGUS WILSON: K. W. Gransden
VIRGINIA WOOLF: B. Blackstone
W. B. YEATS: G. S. Fraser